A Blackbird Sings

A Blackbird Sings

a *small stone* anthology

edited by

Fiona Robyn & Kaspalita Thompson

Woodsmoke Press

A Blackbird Sings
ISBN 978-0-9571584-2-9

Published by Woodsmoke Press 2012
Cover by Ken Hurd
www.kenhurd.com

Woodsmoke Press
37 Clerkenwell Crescent
Malvern
WR14 2TX

kaspa@woodsmokepress.com
www.woodsmokepress.com

For writers of *small stones*, everywhere

"When you notice something clearly and see it vividly, it then becomes sacred."

~ Allen Ginsberg

Contents

Introduction

"The trouble is that essays have to sound like God talking for eternity, and that isn't the way it is. People should see that it's never anything other than just one person talking from one place in time and circumstance."

~ Robert Pirsig

Thank you, reader, for picking up this book. This is the second anthology of *small stones* that Fiona and I have edited together, and it was a real joy to read through all the submissions.

I have some thoughts I'd like to share about what I learnt from the selection process, about what kind of writing makes for good *small stones*, or the kind that *I* like, at least, and about how a carefully crafted *stone* can make both the writer and the reader experience the world in a fresh way.

First though, in the event that you have picked up this volume by chance, I'll say a few words about what *small stones* are and why we think they are important.

A *small stone* is a few words or lines that describe a moment observed: a fragment of prose or poetry that tries to capture something seen, heard, felt, tasted, smelled or experienced in the world. When we write *small stones* we aim for an intimacy with whatever it is that is being observed; we aim for an observation that is as true as possible.

> old eucalyptus continues to slough off his skin,
> long caramel strips hanging down in furled tubes.
> magpie rests in his branches before continuing.
> leaves shift in the circling breezes.

Where did the idea for writing *small stones* come from? I'll let Fiona tell you in her own words:

> In 2005, on a long rainy drive home from the seaside, I thought about my current blog with its long prose pieces and longed instead for somewhere more minimalist, somewhere more sacred. I wanted to create a place where I could really indulge my love of language, and where every word would count. All things begin with a name. I started playing around with labels for this new space. The phrase 'a small stone' floated up from the ether. I dismissed it immediately. It was too plain, too ordinary. I wanted my blog to dazzle, to astonish, to be alive. A part of me wouldn't let it go. It took me on a long beach walk, where my eyes snagged on a smooth pale-blue oval stone. I bent to pick it up and put it in my pocket. I flipped it over, felt the weight of it in my hand, and brushed my fingertips over its granular surface. I stopped looking for a snazzier blog title. Instead I decided to look for a *small stone* every day for a year. That was in 2005, and I'm still going.

Why do we keep writing them and encouraging others to write them? We believe (and have experienced) that it is better to have a close relationship with what is true in the world than a distant one. We believe that a real encountering of the world in all its glory leads to an experience of the world that is more open handed, less judgmental, and more loving. We love writing and we believe that the process of trying to capture these encounters in words can lead to this way of experiencing the world.

In January 2011 we launched the first *River of Stones*. We challenged people everywhere to capture a *small stone* every day for one month. The experience of those writers confirmed our faith in writing *small stones* as a way of connecting people to the world more deeply. It also produced some beautiful writing. Reading those pieces inspired us to create the first anthology of *small stones*.

> "In that month of midwinter gloom, cold grey skies and overwork, every single day, I thought: no, I can't summon the energy to notice something and write it down, and every single day I thought: and what's more, I don't want to. What's the point? And every day I moved through these thoughts and did it, and every day I was enormously glad of such a small thing. Glad because it slowed down time and opened up a space, and something else, however trivial, entered the picture. Glad because a daily practice, as I knew from meditation practice, is a powerfully strengthening, stabilising, calming thing."
>
> ~ Jean Morris, January 2011

We ran the challenge again in the summer of that year, although we didn't produce a collection that time. Instead we edited an issue of *qarrtsiluni*, the online literary journal, an experience that we thoroughly enjoyed. We also got married, and I learnt to drive and started a new job. We like to keep busy.

As I write this, in the midst of our wet English summer, we have a couple of hundred small pieces of paper spread out on our living room floor. These are the *small stones* that you will find in this book chosen from submissions from this year's challenge.

A couple of months ago we were still in the midst of selecting our favourite submissions. Having collected all the submissions and settled into our favourite local café with a sheaf of papers and a slice of carrot cake, we took each *small stone* in turn. When we first looked at each *stone* it was usually easy to make a decision one way or the other, although there was a handful of *stones* that we argued about whether to include.

In this way the selection process was mostly an intuitive one. We both had ideas about what makes a good piece of writing and the kind of writing that we wanted to see in the book, but we didn't talk explicitly about the criteria we were using. I'd like to take some time to think about what made the *small stones* that we chose stand out from the rest.

When I first drafted this introduction I tried to formulate a set of ideas that could be used to help *small stone* writers hone their writing. There is some merit in that approach, and I have written practical hints and tips in other places, but in the final analysis there seems to be something ungraspable at the heart of good writing. Rules (like poetic forms) can help guide us to this place, but they cannot take us all the way.

Having failed in this approach I looked again at the reasons for writing *small stones* that I outlined above (which we first formulated back in January 2011). The making of a good *small stone* must have something to do with those reasons, I thought. How can I talk about the kind of encounter with the world (mediated by, or reflected in, words) that we are working towards?

That question led me to think about four different qualities of a good *small stone*, and I could see that, for me, these qualities had formed a part of the selection criteria for this anthology.

The first three qualities or elements sit together, and I imagine them as a triangle, with each element relating to, and to some extent defining, the others. These are *Truth, Beauty,* and *Love.* The fourth element is to do with both how we experience the world, and how we approach writing *small stones.* I have called this fourth element *Freshness.*

Truth, beauty, and love are inherently good qualities to cultivate in one's life. Can we meet the world, another person, and ourselves, in a true way? Can we see such a thing as having its own beauty? Can we receive it in a more loving way? I believe that writing *small stones* is one route towards this way of being.

Truth

Does the *small stone* I am reading point to an authentic experience? On a gross level, if I read a *small stone* and think something is factually wrong I might ask if it is a mistake, or if the writer is seeing something in the world that I am not. Are the lavender flowers really a deep red? Perhaps they are lit by a setting sun...

The factual truth of a *small stone* will be easier for the writer to check than the reader. Who knows if it was really a lapwing that you saw? Only you.

Something factually false might still point to a particular truth. We might write of a fictional lapwing in order to get close to the sense of longing as the lapwing flies away, becoming at first a dot, and then nothing — and the desire in my heart to follow.

In that sense my experience of the truth of a *small stone* happens on a deep, intuitive level. It comes out of my experience of being in the world, and of being human. The more aware I am of my own humanity, of the currents of feeling that move through me, of the cracks in my soul, and of my own longing to keep encountering the world in a vivid way, the more of the truth of others I can intuit and encompass.

> She wanders away from her parents. I follow her outside. Together we chase after a blackbird. She blows kisses at it. The blackbird flies a little way off, we follow. A little way off. We follow. Suddenly she looks around and there is a big field of grass between her and her mummy. Until they are back in sight I can't stop her tears.
> ~ Fiona Robyn

This *small stone* from Fiona strikes me as true in both of these ways. Factually, even if I had not been there, I know this is the kind of thing that happens when children stray too far from their parents. For me this also points to a broader experience of separation that goes beyond this one specific incident. This specific moment in time is a window into a more universal human experience — and for me it works precisely because it is showing us a particular moment in time.

Beauty

In terms of *small stone* writing, we can think of finding beauty in two places. The first is in what we encounter in the world, and the second is in the language we use to transmit that beauty in our *small stone*.

How beautiful a piece of writing is depends on all the different cultures that I inhabit, as well as on my own personal sense of aesthetics. Perhaps it also depends on something ungraspable. Later I will talk about how we can move towards seeing more and more things as beautiful but it is also true that each of us will prefer some things over other things. Each of us will prefer some writing over other writing (although experience suggests there will also be plenty of overlap). We often make these kinds of judgements without being able to say precisely what beauty is.

There is something about the beauty of the written word that resists analysis. There are many different ways of critiquing a text, windows we can look through that give a particular view of what makes beautiful reading, but there is no universal rule that we can apply. Iris Murdoch has written about the tendency in Western philosophy to want to reduce what the good life is to a single rule and I recognise this tendency in myself. If I can find a simple way of approaching life (or writing) that I can apply universally, then everything will be good. If only I could find that one rule!

In writing, as in life, there is more than one way to make something beautiful. However I do have a sense that

> Chickweed grows through the discarded bricks: ochre, burnt umber, cracked and crumbling. They glow in the dusk.

Is more beautifully written than

> A pile of bricks.

Not only do I think that the first is more beautifully written, I also have a sense that the writer of the first *small stone* has appreciated the beauty of the scene more than the writer of the second.

17

Love

As one's writing becomes more in tune with the truths of one's experience, the more one is able to see the beauty in that moment, and the more love one feels for all the myriad things in the world.

You may encounter something classically beautiful: a lotus flower, a swallow-tail butterfly, or a blackbird singing. You may encounter something that falls outside what we usually think of as beautiful: the squashed corpse of a fox on the roadside, litter blowing through an underpass, or the stain of mildew on a damp wall. We could argue about which items on those two lists might be beautiful, but I believe that if we can encounter them all with an open heart something beautiful will emerge. We begin to notice all the shades of green on the closed flower buds, and the patterns the wind makes in the grass. It is this kind of encounter I am talking about when I use the word *love*: a way of being in the world that is sympathetic to others and carries less judgement and less conceit. For example this:

> He stumbles at the edge of the pavement and refuses to catch my eye. The paper bag he carries creases in the tight grip of one hand, the other is stuffed deep into a pocket. The wind musses his hair, and he shuffles on.

is probably better than this:

> The old drunk can't walk.

These three elements, as I have described them, seem to be fundamental to what makes a good *small stone*. Deciding which of the submissions epitomised these three elements was a subjective and intuitive experience, but I am confident that each of the *small stones* in this book are truthful, beautiful, and full of love in the sense I have described.

Freshness

What I mean by freshness is considering something ordinary in an extraordinary way — the art of making readers see what you are writing about as if they are seeing it or hearing it for the first time. Does your *small stone* draw readers into the experience of being with the blackbird on the chimney pot in an intimate way?

> Around his eye, a yellow ring (a shade paler than his beak). The blackbird is on the roof, in the shadow of a Staffordshire-blue chimney. He drops his half-worm, dips, picks it up, and flies away.

This idea of freshness is another window to view *small stones* through. I think that *small stones* which accomplish this also tend to capture the three elements that I spoke of earlier. You have to really look at what you are writing about, and encounter it fully, in order to make your *small stone* come alive for the reader. When you start to encounter the world in this way, your *small stones* will also come to embody *truth, beauty* and *love.*

How alive a *small stone* appears on the page has something to do with how it is written and something to do with the subjective life of the reader. I am reminded of sages in my own Buddhist tradition who had powerful enlightenment experiences after reading something, but the next person who read those same words experienced nothing.

You might have a very powerful experience of 'being with' the blackbird on the chimney pot and capture something of that experience in words. Sometimes your words will inspire the same kind of experience in me, and sometimes they won't.

What is it that makes the difference?

The word *cliché* comes from the French word for a printing plate (also called a stereotype) used to reproduce the same set of words over and over again. If you were to read every copy of a single pamphlet produced by one of these movable type machines, you would receive the same words, the same images and ideas, hundreds of times. Having heard the same ideas over and over again your mind is turned off; it shuts down.

It is in reacting against cliché that literature is driven forward.

That imaginary pamphlet produced by the stereotype machine may have been inspired by a completely new thought, or a new configuration of ideas that hadn't been seen before. But even those inspired thoughts become old news when they filter down (through word of mouth, or through being appropriated by other writers) into everyone's minds.

What if you haven't read any of these ideas from the imaginary pamphlet, or heard any of these words, and the insight comes freshly to you? You want to share it and write something of your own, but when you take it to the people who have already heard all about it, you won't be able to excite many of them. If, on the other hand, you put your words in front of someone to whom they are new, she or he will probably experience some of the same excitement you first felt when you wrote those words down.

It's the same with *small stones* as it is with these imaginary pamphlets. And if we really look at what excites people, it is not the completely new but something just on the boundary between the known and the unknown. Something completely new is confusing and unintelligible. Something completely

20

known is dead. In this way artistic movements inch forwards a little at a time.

All of which supports the idea that the experience of freshness is something to do with both the reader and the writer and the cultures that both inhabit.

My culture as a reader includes all the *small stones* that people have written for our previous challenges as well as all the other works of prose and poetry that I have absorbed.

When we are writing we can think of freshness as having two elements. There is the written form of the piece (formal vs. informal, verbose vs. concise) and also the content. As a reader, if I find something *fresh* in the content *or* the form it might be enough to excite me — to bring a sense of the intimacy of encounter with what is being described.

The *small stones* challenge usually runs in January, and many of our submissions come from the Northern Hemisphere. This year and last year we received lots of submissions about snow. If you write about snow, you need to take care with *how* you write about it. Can the words you use bring readers to a place where they can really feel the stiffening of their scarves as they clog with lumps of dirty snow and the dampness of their skin as those clots of snow melt around their shoulders?

If you write about something less usually observed, that aliveness might jump off the page simply by virtue of what it is you are talking about: A grease-smeared chip packet in the gutter. A shadow of a dead moth inside a light. A dripping wad of blood-soaked gauze in a surgeon's steel bowl.

Both form and content can become stale, but if you can energise one of these two components you have my interest.

For example: in contemporary literary journals it's difficult to get poems with end rhymes published. The poetry world has seen so many of these and often the first rhyming word

21

we reach for is already overused... This isn't to say that you shouldn't use end rhymes at all, but that it's harder to make them really jump off the page. How can you bring new life to something stale? Write a rhyming poem about something unusual: The queue at the dole office; or the way the light moves across your sitting room floor, bringing to life the dust, the cat-hairs, and last night's half eaten pizza. Or search for end-rhymes that we haven't heard before.

When we were choosing *small stones* for this collection I held these ideas of form/content in mind. We have fifty submissions about song-birds, how many should go in the book?

When I spoke to Fiona about these ideas around freshness she asked me about particular pieces of writing that we go back to again and again — those poems or sections of novels we love with a deeper affection each time we read them. Although we are reading the same ideas in the same form, we keep going back to them. How does this fit in with my thoughts on freshness?

I'll try to answer this from my own experience of reading and loving the same poems over and over again. Each time I go to them I experience something new. For me this happens in two different ways.

The first time I read a poem by Rumi, for example, I am struck by the truth of what he writes and become determined to live my life with the same intensity and devotion he displays.

Our personalities are pernicious and tend towards stability. The effects of writing that challenges us to change, to see the world in a new way, can fade away as our personality re-asserts itself and we fall back into old ways. When I read the Rumi poem again, it is as if I am reading it for the first time. In this way I am experiencing the same thing as new all over again.

The second way of experiencing something as new more than once is that when I read a text multiple times, each time it points to something different. This is partly because I am coming to the text as a new person — I *have* changed since the last time I read the poem, and I bring these experiences to the reading — and partly because the poem itself may be describing something which is hard to grasp.

Earlier I said that art which exists in the boundary between the known and the unknown is the kind of art that excites us. The world is not easily understood. Great literature opens us up to greater meaning and continually points us to what is not containable by words. These texts that we return to over and over again are like doorways into an experience that is always on the boundary between what is known and what is unknown (how can love be completely explained?). This is where some of their power comes from.

If a text does this very well, each time we read it we are directed into something completely beyond ourselves. Each time we have this kind of encounter we are exposed to new layers of meaning or new forms of old truths (the feeling of love is universal, the feeling of loving someone in particular is unique).

The freshness here occurs in the encounter between who I am in that moment and something much greater than I. Good *small stones,* whilst a thing of beauty in themselves, also point beyond themselves into the world and can engender this kind of encounter.

When I go back to a favourite text, my experience is often a mixture of these two experiences: a little of "ahh, I'd forgotten that" and a little of "oh, I'd never thought of that".

In choosing which *small stones* to include in this anthology one thing that I asked was, "Does this *small stone* come alive for me? Does it speak in a fresh way? Does it tell me something new (or something I had forgotten) about the world?"

I hope my thoughts about these four elements — *truth, beauty, love,* and *freshness* — will help you to appreciate the *small stones* in this collection. I also hope they might help you in some of your own writing adventures.

My final suggestions for writing your own *small stones*: read lots of them, savour the ones in this collection, let your view of the world be opened up a little, and think about the words you use to reflect the world. Begin to take steps from the known towards the infinite.

> A thin band of light between the sea and the grey sky. The dawn is softly golden.

Kaspalita
September 2012

Kaspa has written eloquently about our process of choosing *small stones* for this book, and on what criteria we might make those choices. His musings have brought to my mind the apparent incompatibility of our two main goals:

1. We want people to feel free to write, regardless of whether they see themselves as 'proper writers' (whatever that might mean) and regardless of the quality of their writing.
2. We want people to write well.

Most of us struggle to write creatively. Even a single *small stone* a day can be a real challenge. This is because most of us, with the exception of a few annoying people whom I won't mention here, have to do constant battle with our internal critics. These internal critics tell us that we are god-awful writers, and that we shouldn't dream of inflicting our writing on other people, and that it would really be better if we didn't write anything in the first place.

As well as being a writer, I am a psychotherapist. In the therapy room, I am inviting people to say the things that they have been unable to say to anyone else. This is not easy. These things have often been driven far underground, and are terribly tangled up with shame and fear. So much so, that my clients are often surprised to hear these things themselves.

The conditions that make this gradual and courageous unfolding possible are, as the psychotherapist Carl Rogers would list them, *congruence*, *empathy*, and *unconditional positive regard*. Another way of putting this: I need to be my authentic self, I need to fully comprehend what it might be like to be my client, and I need to accept everything my client says or reveals or does with warmth and love (whilst holding appropriate boundaries for myself, of course).

Unconditional positive regard. Not conditional positive regard for all the bits of my clients that I like the best.

Most of us have very sensitive antennae when it comes to being judged. Any judgement is a shutting out of a part of our selves. We already feel awful enough about these parts of us, and so the prospect of being rejected as a result of their unacceptability is almost unbearable.

The unfortunate truth is that we can't just snip these parts of ourselves away. Yes, it might not be pleasant to acknowledge that you're always greedy for more money or that you're jealous of the attention your son receives from your wife, but the only way to begin to change is to welcome in these greedy or jealous parts of you and to love them as they are.

There is a part of me that wants to say yes to every *small stone* we receive. Apart from making for a very big and prohibitively heavy book, would there be anything wrong with this? Isn't this what I do in the therapy room?

Maybe unconditional positive regard isn't the whole picture. Once the client's material has entered the room, once we have welcomed it, then we do look at it with a critical eye. You say your mother hated you. Is this really true? Is 'morose' the best word for how you feel, or is 'desolate' more accurate? When you talk about your brother's negative attitude, what reaction comes up inside me as the therapist — annoyance? Boredom? What does this reaction tell us about the way you form relationships with others and with the world?

Without this feedback, without my clients coming–up–against–something and us being curious about the effects of this contact, I don't think therapeutic work would be possible. I don't think growth would be possible. Maybe Rogers was right in that we should be aiming towards unconditional positive regard. But maybe conditional positive regard is also an essential part of the mix. We don't have to worry about cultivating this quality, because as human beings our love usually (always?) comes with conditions attached.

So what does any of this have to do with putting words onto paper?

Writers such as Dorothea Brande talk about writing as consisting of two distinct phases. The first is where we get the writing *out*. We get words out of our head and onto the page. The best way to do this is to welcome them all, unconditionally. We acknowledge that, as Anne Lamott says, our first draft is likely to be pretty shitty.

The second phase is where we engage our critical mind and become discerning. Would our prose be improved by line breaks? Does the staccato rhythm of that first line enhance or detract from our meaning? Do we really need that middle section where we got a bit carried away with a long list of birds? Some people are lucky enough to write beautifully without any revising. But for most of us, this phase is like polishing a dirty mirror. It allows our writing to shine.

I think my aims as a therapist and our two goals with *small stones* can both be mapped onto this model.

Our first goal is in encouraging people to just speak or to just write, without any fear of being judged. Just observe, record, let your pen run away with you. Don't worry about whether it's any good or not. Everything is welcome.

Our second goal is to help people grow as people and as writers. This requires some discernment and some boundaries. It requires a little pain. It's why I've written and re-written and re-written this introductory essay, so it (hopefully) makes more sense and reads more fluently. This is why we've chosen our favourite *small stones* to go into this book. We hope that reading these exquisitely polished *small stones* will inspire you to keep on polishing your own, and to raise your bar.

I will love and accept every *small stone* that you will ever write, whether or not you send it to me. And I also have favourites. I have favourites because I am a human being, thank goodness. And so are you.

Unconditional and conditional. Both these things are true at the same time. I wouldn't have it any other way.

Fiona Robyn
September 2012

"It's not necessary to connect with the stars to go beyond our own boundaries. We can realise increased awareness in smaller steps: hearing the song of a bird, looking into the eyes of a newborn, sharing another's pain."

~ Ezra Bayda

By bronze barrows,
my foot falls on
a path cut through
five thousand summers

Doug Robertson

A sail-less charcoal windmill casts a shadow
over bullrushes flapping in the canal.
A seagull on the wing of a burning cloud.

Martin Cordrey

Caught in the beam of the headlights
leaves scuttle across the road like mice.

Elizabeth Leaper

Olive leaves reflect
the sun like slim, silver fish,
swimming in bright shoals.

Kathleen Jones

Last night's steady rain brought:
Smelly dogs on wet blankets,
(Why do they carry their blankets out into the rain?)
Mud oozing up between patio blocks,
Musty cigarette smoke smells from a million years ago,
The smoker doin' her dyin'.
But inside the grocery store:
Gerber daisies, Valentine's candy and Easter foreplay
Parley beneath florescent lights.

Trinity Sigler Nicholas

Sidewalks are wearing their necklaces
of brown water, puddled in the pits and cracks,
reflecting nothing:
tenements and spires are wearing headdresses
of fog.

Joseph Harker

Branches. D of a dawn-moon's a leaf alight.

Liam Wilkinson

Black polythene, the wind's booty from its mad escapade,
twitches in the bare branches of the silver birch.

Lindsay Stanberry-Flynn

The Brussels Sprout plants are mesmerised by the winter's
first frost; their silver tipped leaves and elegant stalks
statuesque above soil darkened by cold.

Marilyn Hammick

who notices the thinner-than-usual
ice on the pond?
the mallard that waddles,
then unexpectedly swims.

Becky Feltmeyer

stillness again ~
it curls around the room like a
plume of August river smoke

Becky Feltmeyer

river at low tide:
mud and stones and plastic bags,
the gulls gather

Jean Morris

On the lawn some grackles are milling
mobbing and strutting flaunting their tails
like soiled shiny suspect flags.

Gregory Luce

A plumped up pigeon
Pecks around a puddle
Purple grey on slate grey

Sheree Mack

It
fell
as he took
to the sky
twisting & spinning
its own separate trail
this mystery of nature –
just quill and some barbs
such a small, seemingly
fragile bit of nothing
the finest of filaments,
practically transparent
assisting flight, providing
warmth and decoration
its amazing blue (like the
moon's glow) merely
a reflection
nothing
more

Pamela Smyk Cleary

The cat has been scratching the couch again,
and we know from finding his old claw sheaths,
those shed chitinous commas,
which I gathered, and used, to populate
this poem.

Joseph Harker

i watch my cat wash,
his tongue is a bubblegum elastoplast,
his little paw like segments of pink plasticine,
his concentration uncluttered, intense,
eyes wide as green marbles,
only stopping for an instant to glare accusingly at his tail.

Mark Sargeant

holding #8 steel blue knitting needles, 40 garter stitches, nothing fancy. I'm making a scarf, I'm always making a scarf and it doesn't seem to really matter that I don't have a finished product. That's not why I knit. Right now, it's mostly about bringing my mind into the present moment, staying aware of my breath...breathing in bring right needle under loop on left needle, loop yarn around, over, feel the drag of the wool yarn across my index finger, pull the needle through and voila! another stitch is born...breathing out start again. Keep the yarn just so...not too taut, not too loose...the middle way...keeping the hands busy, the mind occupied, the shoulders down and relaxed, the head tipped slightly down but not strained. I think I love to knit.

Mary Sherman

plump rolls of new toilet paper—
I place them on the étagère
with pleasure, the way I place fresh fruit
on the counter, on the fruit tray

Michelle Angeles

white dog settle-sighs
red throw underneath
sour-stinks

Elizabeth Kate Switaj

Down to bare bones in January, I get a glimpse of the
inevitable.

Susan Elbe

shoveling snow
for the last time
again

Daphne Ashling Purpus

Just ahead,
in the white on white of blowing snow,
a little arctic fox slips across the road like a ghost.

Cathy Rose

"It's possible, in a poem or short story, to write about commonplace things and objects using commonplace but precise language, and to endow those things—a chair, a window curtain, a fork, a stone, a woman's earring—with immense, even startling power."

~ Raymond Carver

Flash of iridescence as two magpies squabble in the winter
sun
and I drive home from hospital with the news you might not
make it.

Emma Lee

Whisper thin translucent twists, spread out across a vast
expanse of blue, fine strands twirl as unruly as golden locks of
hair.

Kay Beer

Twenty-four hours
since you died
the sun still moves
across the sky

Allyson Whipple

tea for one...
stirring in the emptiness with a spoon

Sanjukta Asopa

all day long
the barometric
pressure falls;
my fingers fumble
with the chopsticks

Aubrie Cox

she's been gone over ten years
it's been raining for days
today gray lays on gray
and all I wish for is the smell
of wet dog

Terri L. French

With an ice pack folded over my knees, I watch the girl next to
me pinch her toes around a glass marble, pick it up and drop it
into a ceramic coffee cup on the floor.

Jeannine Peregrine

christmas packed in four boxes.
the tree as bare as it came.

Nan Pasquarello

A New Year

dawn arrives
on the maple
seventy times seven
crescent moons germinate
in dewdrops

Kay Tracy

New Year's Day —
rain falls
from last year's clouds

Lonnard Dean Watkins

cocoa and kirsch
shielding us
from the cold
we speak between scrabble turns
about the loss of our mothers

Kat Creighton

The express train passes us,
two tracks over: steel piers and
beveled squares of light suggest
momentary aqueducts,
a Roman ruin half-wrapped
in blind noise.

Joseph Harker

first day back
s h a t t e r e d
w i ne gl a s   s

Mat Cross

Waxing Moon

Molten gold at the bottom of a rippling river,
a quarter moon smoldering
through the juniper branches.

Lorna Cahall

The sky is pulling its
coral crimson shades on the day
and my stone remains unturned, unlearned
sleepwalked over through faded fog.

All that remains:
this simple sliver of gray slate
overturned by wayward toe
dropped at river's edge.

De Jackson

The moon followed me home again tonight, peeked through
my window as I got ready for bed, then silently sank into the
horizon as I drifted off to sleep.

gibbous moon
the night light in the hallway
burns out

Stevie Strang

moonlight
waiting for one more
poem

Christina Nguyen

god
I need a cigarette
or something
close to it

Lucas Stensland

smoking on her front porch
in the early morning,
the old woman inhales sharply —
frowning prisoner of her own addiction.

Nan Pasquarello

the heron, a black silhouette against the grey morning sky
flapping slowly, fighting the wind, veering, heading south
I watch until my arms ache from holding a basket
of wet washing that needs to be hung on the line

Freya Pickard

The wood pile holds treasures... The shed skin of a snake
And the soft chewed woven grass of an abandoned squirrels
        nest
And spores of mushrooms that have settled and grown.

JulesPaige/davh

The strange flower of a child's glove shrieking in pink from the hawthorn bush.

Liam Wilkinson

Sounds in the Barn:

The hissing of the horse's hip, rubbing rubbing rubbing on wood is just loud enough to echo in the quiet and scratch at my nerves. Since the mare is wearing her green winter coat, the sound is more like 'zzz' 'zzz' 'zzz' and I rub at my raw hands. I can't sit and listen so I grab a broom. It is so cold that the wood is like ice. The 'shh' 'shh' 'shh' of the broom matches the hissing. Suddenly she stops, shakes herself, and I can just see her dark nose through the bars. She sniffs the air, smelling me.

Elise Geither

kissed by summer evening light
even this cow pat
is beautiful

Helen Lewis

The fence ran up the hill.
Carrying shadows
along for the ride.

Teri Hoover

Safe from the night's frost in their white woolly fleeces, the
ghosts of the bay tree and the bottle brush haunt the garden.

Lindsay Stanberry-Flynn

At night, the rain's desultory percussion.
And, through an imperfectly-fitting window frame, the
mournful harmonica of the wind.

Mark Holloway

"...we may notice amazing details during the course of a day but we rarely let ourselves stop and really pay attention. An author *makes* you notice, makes you pay attention, and this is a great gift."

~ Anne Lamott

The trees are just appearing against the lightening dawn sky.
The ravens are speaking. They started their conversation in
the dark.

Kit Cooley

Shimmering sunlight shines straight, through tangled skeletal
hedgerows, serrated by fine twigs & twisted gnarled
branches.

Kay Beer

It is sunset. Crows speak in black-wing
on sky-fire; above the pines,
First United Church GOD
IS LOVE BINGO SUPPER SUNDAY.
Everywhere there are signs. Houses. Ca$h.
No quick closings, nor wonder
in fortified bread.

Kitty Jospé

moonlight haze
we watch cars whisper
through the night

James Brush

Zumba class
the old Cuban man
danced his salsa his way

Mary-Jane Grandinetti

An evening duet

out of time with the
dishwasher's two-tone samba
a lark is singing

Helen Lewis

enjoying the rain
    without an umbrella
        I run in and out
            of the shelter of trees
                pausing to thank them

Susan Rogers

winter in bucketloads
tiptoe! my bike's wheels will fearlessly dare all the puddles
under the spell of my new hat

Dora Bampali

Bitter wind ruffles free range feathers, as a low winter sun
casts long shadows across the fields.

Rebecca Emin

along the interstate,
sabal palmettos on wood tripods—
a thick weave of left-off brown boots
below a crown of green fans
on every slender trunk

Michelle Angeles

Bruised Skies

The new moon, the size and shape of a slim cuticle, here in
this part of the hemisphere, shows as a sly grin against
Arizona's bruised sunset skies — all mauves, dove-grey and
faint apricot bleeding out ...

S.E. Ingraham

Bits of color on bits of paper. Lines carved deep in hazel wood.
The sun along the slant of a cloud. A blackbird lifting to join a
friend in the air.

Kate Dooley

Vision board: layers of phases & phrases, moments & mementoes — trampling one another for attention; a curling sticker from one of the kids; a bunch of photoshop-bright ranunculus

Kylie Andersen

Dark and bright Mexico, with its sad dogs and jewel-like stitching, the smells of sewers drowned by the sites of ancient spirit and sweet–eyed children.

Fran Riley

The shadow of the mesquite tree:
like a paper cut-out against black asphalt.

Carla M. Wilson

The white truck rumbles
down the road,
full of artichokes.

Richard Cody

In front of the barn
Two fat hens scratch in Autumn's leaves
One runs away with a wiggling worm...

Patricia B. Sawyer

creeping sunshine -
all along the rooftops
a breath of gold

Jean Morris

He said we'd have to eat the sun
five layers, downhill to the core
yellow bell peppers... or orange?
Sour cream and, and some Cool Whip... dyed!
Shredded carrots; no, no...mandarin oranges!
How about some cake frosting, too?
We better buy a lot of food coloring
for this freak of a model
oh, and a sliver of cottage cheese
moon on the side
don't you think?

Laurie Kolp

At the checkout line, a toddler with angel hair sits in the cart, counting the letters of the store's name printed on the handle. Twisting backward, he hands each item to the clerk, and watches enthralled as she pours Mama's coffee beans into the grinder. And I think, for him it's all small stones.

Cathy Douglas

"Look Mama, do you see the bronze in the sky?" *He was right.*
The clouds were bronze. "If you look at them with your eyes
open, they are bronze. When you close your eyes, they are still
there. Only they are green and bright yellow." *He was right*
again. We stood on the morning sidewalk, holding the clouds
inside our eyelids.

Suzanne Stauss

shooting star -
a baby slithers out
of the womb

Stella Pierides

In my dream
the small stones grow
to make a crossing-place

Hilaire Wood

Morning sun bathes sand in gentle amber. The shore is a slab of caramel, frosted in foam and dusted with the footprints of gulls.

Claire Marriott

take-off
a young child screams
all the way to the clouds

Mat Cross

At breakfast
the one-year-old
crawls through the tunnel
of cafeteria chairs.
His father deep in conversation
and all the women watching.

Robin Chapman

I describe my car's strange noise
to the mechanic,
who nods, and repeats:

the oscillating black fan with a wire cage...
the sound the blade makes with a carving fork?

I got it.

Barbara Young

leftover shards of
rain – rhyming cars trickle down

the soft drizzly street

Dora Bampali

Three nearly-full hard-drives;
Chrome watch, clasp left open;
A battered brown leather wallet;

Half-eaten packet of Orbit chewing gum;
Invoice for £45, number 015;
Nine wires, mostly black and two white

Adrian Thompson

Slugs surface at night
Sliding into damp tiled outhouses
Silvering floors.

Helen Bayly

HYDRANGEA

Four shavings of sky
perfect blue
held in place by
a tiny French knot

Claire Zoghb

"I'm saying look, here they come, pay attention. Let your eyes transform what appears ordinary, commonplace, into what it is, a moment in time, an observed fragment of eternity."

~ Philip Levine

Into a bright blue January sky, I let the pale moon travel to its
furthest extent.
The wind zithers the strings that connect us.

Mark Holloway

Unexpected vista

torn paper hills
in layers of deepening blue
one pink cloud

Helen Lewis

Nestled in the shelter of a mossy stone,
Green spikes poke through dead leaf litter,
Delicate white flowers touched with lime
Dip their heads, hang like shy lampshades,
I bend my knees and crouch
To look into their light.

Cilla Sparks

Greening footholds on the yew and a rope that once held a swing. This white winter day's a page of deletions.

Liam Wilkinson

Trees bend to the will of the wind, the grey skies crowding out the daylight in this dreary English winter. Rain lashes against the window pane like a soft rap of knuckles demanding attention. The streetlights signal an early surrender to the gathering gloom. Summer seems an impossible dream.

Peter Domican

I'm drunk on hammock-worthy sunshine that saturates me in heat, bone-deep, so when I have to open my eyes, it's like raising plutonium.

Lanita Andrews

It is January in the North, but Spring
is dancing an exclamation point!
Straight down, puddling to point
in the non-snowy ground.
It's a scrabble of jazz-knuckled plants
trading in teasel and burdock nettled-to-brittle
for fresh green weeds.

Kitty Jospé

Blue tits busy in the gauze of the passiflora that curtains my
door.
Young wheat rests in sun-touched fields, like a bolt of green
taffeta
spread for consideration on a dressmaker's bench; close up
new shoots
dance on their points.

Marilyn Hammick

Jacaranda showers
purple rain
on a thirsty garden

Merlene Fawdry

A pigeon sits immobile on the wall, beneath palm leaves made ragged by a week of hard buffeting. Its eyes, black, map-pin orbs, in an amber sea, are fixed on the bearded bark. Perhaps it contemplates a warm nest lined with the fibrous thatch, or is just wondering how alien the tree looks here in the eastern shires. A sharp gust ruffles the bird's composure. Chest feathers puff up like a lilac pillow, reflecting the strange paint choice on the courtyard wall.

Lesley Hale

A constellation of seven yellow limes rests on dark green grass.

Laura L Mays Hoopes

My sister's baby called me yesterday. She is almost a year old, and must have pressed the redial button. I said, hello? hello? But she was talking about something I couldn't understand. I held on the phone until I didn't hear her anymore. I hope she calls again. Because I will listen.

Dawn Apanius

she is laughing when she says she lost her coat; now she's angry because I'm angry and we both hang up the phone. I hear a little girl wrapped in a woman's voice and there is nothing I can do to keep her warm.

Angie Werren

gold moon
my nose pressed against
cold glass

Kirsten Cliff

Blonde on a coat,
a lash of light. I close my eyes,
this crescent moon
not exactly where I left it.

Angela Readman

My husband slices the serranos, and the air splits and burns with the breath of the chiles.

Ruth Feiertag

sniff, snort, swallow
breathe, gag, hack
the mucous monologue
of sinusoidal life

Dr S

I take small nibbles of the crisp chocolate chip cookie. While this method helps me to savor the delicious treat, it does not mean that I will eat only one.

Tasleem Khan

Morning surprise ~ a white heart center in the kiwi halves.

Linda Hofke

a summer's night
a country lane
in the glare of my headlights
a gentle snowfall of moths

Helen Lewis

windshield rain
roadside deer skeleton
in lush grass

James Brush

A tiny grey speckled bird's egg lies in the garden bed.
But for a small hole at one end, the shell is whole.
When I pick up the delicate casing, a single ant emerges.
The empty shell is heavier than it should be, so I check.
A desiccated embryo is stuck to the inside wall,
And weighs down the egg at its little end.

Linda Visman

a thought while swimming:
to be
like water

Dorothee Lang

I hold hands while the small, disaffected rider
trails, sighing, far behind.

Jean Morris

first poetry reading
the silent crowd
of teddy bears

Christina Nguyen

the station is a chorus of polished announcements, blue sky
and yellow train doors

Kylie Andersen

"I have to use that thingy
on the windshield."
Californian sister.
Can't remember the word
for ice scraper.

Connie L. Peters

frost bite
the winter bares its teeth

Stella Pierides

a text message
illuminates a cat's yawn
daybreak

Lucas Stensland

catching snowflakes
on my tongue
hot tub soak

Daphne Ashling Purpus

A Snail On Easter Road

A patient God in the rain;
oblivious to the business shoes.

Like the gentle progress
of an ocealiner across the Atlantic.

The smallest most slow of comets
glittering a trail across wet night pavement

Colin McGuire

sparrows

spa r   r   o   w   s

silence

CAT

R.G. Rader

"But if you really learn how to pay attention, then you will know there are other options. It will actually be within your power to experience a crowded, hot, slow, consumer-hell type situation as not only meaningful, but sacred, on fire with the same force that made the stars: love, fellowship, the mystical oneness of all things deep down.

"Not that that mystical stuff is necessarily true. The only thing that's capital-T True is that you get to decide how you're gonna try to see it."

~ David Foster Wallace

this colored joy
of buying pink tulips
in january

Dorothee Lang

Yellow tulips dip over the rim of my vase like ballerinas
bowing for applause.

Rosalind Adam

a voice that stays
and follows you around
strong stale onions on your hand

Barbara Young

In the winter-killed remains of the vegetable
garden, a half-row of Swiss Chard is still
producing. I remove a handful of mulch
and there they are — little nests of curly,
bright green leaves. And they still taste good!

Marian Veverka

in the basket of her hands
she holds a gray bird
until it flies off to the apple tree

Renee Cassese

blue goat's cheese —
a moon waiting
for a silvered cut

Jenny Hope

I slice the cucumber so thinly the light shines through. My knife slips. I should hide the half slices but where? In my mouth!

Rosalind Adam

Never mind that we've had this dishwasher several
         years
I still step back to avoid the dripping from the door
of the previous one.

Sandra Davies

shrimp, pale pink apostrophes arranged on the plate

Jeannine Peregrine

January light—
dust on the window
freckles the plate
on our table.

Angela Readman

Crumbs from cinnamon raisin toast, left a moment too long in
the toaster, dot the small white plate. Black crumbs, brown
crumbs. Big, tiny. Clumped, solo. But no Virgin Mary.

Kathy Wiederin

Peeled from its banana leafed wrappings, this lightly
sweetened & fried banh chung fills in the gaps between
fullness & emptiness.

Kathy Uyen Nguyen

I split the scarlet pod with a sharp blade and scrape the seeds out with a single movement. One sliced seed sticks against the steel, its matt velvet in startling contrast to the sheen of polished metal. My eyes water from the stinging vapours or from the small cut that weeps deep scarlet blood.

Martin Porter

Today the grey umbrella of cloud has closed everything in. Rain pools on white marble like spilt milk.

Kathleen Jones

He is selling frozen eels from a box in the market square, smashing them into smaller pieces with a hammer.

Bob Hale

January's gloom
I put the tea kettle on
just to hear it whistle

Terri L. French

If I had to be a god, I'd be
god of the scent of pumpkin bread,
holding back the cold
with enviable spice.

Joseph Harker

SUN (LIKE CLOCKWORK):
The sky is pinking up this morning beyond the screen of bare
trees at the end of my street, extinguishing the street lamps,
proving that the sun always rises, even when it's twelve
degrees out, even when Joan learned last night that her
mother has one, at best two, weeks to live. The sun is
stubborn like that, insisting and insisting, shedding light
wherever it pleases, even when it's not wanted.

Laurie Granieri

creek water slides across the road where it curves into a one-lane bridge. the peacocks are out, and it's hard to tell which are leucistic and which are just covered with snow. I imagine their missing tail feathers, the unexpected white slowly melting into iridescent color.

Angie Werren

For Dad:

We smooth the sheets,
speak kind words, softly,
and hope for your light in the dark.

Sara D. Thibault

two restless and sleepless nights —
from my patio door
the burnt scarlet of the sunrise

Mary-Jane Grandinetti

                    within
              the swirling
        sandalwood smoke

someone plays a flute

                    outside
                    it is winter
                    s t i l l

Johannes S. H. Bjerg

The new-year sun, burning through the old-year clouds,
slickering the empty streets.

Susan Elbe

wild gusts from the west
strum low notes on the power lines

Sue Spencer

The ibis,
   long legs half-vanished
     in these impromptu lakes,
like lanky spear-fishers
   before the sails and shackles,
dance
   and probe
     at what the rain washed out
and do not turn
   to watch
     the train roar past.

mr oCean

He sleeps pale
translucent,
wakes to talk of dying.

When I tickle him,
blood returns
with his laughter.

Rosemary Nissen-Wade

82

prayer flags...
a rainbow of family washcloths hangs
on the shower rod

Christina Nguyen

a cold night—
dipping the spoon and taking up
what's left of the warm soup
carrying the tray into the kitchen
rinsing this bowl

Michelle Angeles

Nostalgia

You've made me think again of the time,
when nothing more terrible happened
than missing the last bus home and walking
in the dead night dreaming up excuses.

Kate Noakes

a welcoming

not yet risen,
the sun throws rose-petal clouds
across the sky.

Cynthia Sidrane

The door blows open
sunlight
rolls a golden carpet down the hall

Hilaire Wood

Today wags in loose skins
like my old-dog-sag-wagon
rattling love-cracked lungs
against her ribs. Suddenly,
she bursts into song,
pinning scents
in the key of B.

Kitty Jospé

empty glass
the sound
of his sobs

Kirsten Cliff

The pain comes and goes
like the tide.
In, and out.
In, and out.

Allyson Whipple

Soft Mother

Breathing into the dark
night flows across my shoulder—
a gray cat licking her kitten.

Lorna Cahall

We met at someone's house on Lake Placid later that summer, you from Canada and me from Rhode Island. Lying in someone else's big bed, you noticed that my thighs were slightly bigger. *You're generally too scrawny,* you said, *I like it this way.* I held onto the spindles, scratched a mosquito bite, made a cross with my nail to stop the itch.

Elizabeth Aquino

pillow mint
our eyes meet
before I swallow

Andrea Grillo

snowmelt—
Turkish jazz drifts in
with the afternoon

Aubrie Cox

pink mist floats
around Mount Tam
Sunday eases out
perfectly

Julie Gengo

Wind tosses a pinch
of black birds across clear blue
seasoning the sky

Claire Zoghb

empty park bench
a hawk glides overhead
long winter shadows

James Brush

"There's a great deal to say about how we tend to see, and hear, only what has been pointed out to us . . . We are given words for those things that are pointed out to us. What about everything else? What are we missing?"
~ Pattiann Rogers

it wasn't on
my 'to do' list...
listening
to a robin

Paul Smith

spring breeze —
a cottonwood tree
speaks brook

Craig W. Steele

Snake and Bird

In the winter landscape
the snake with his skin of leaves and grass
hunts the water bird.

Catherine Arcolio

the road
creeps across the contours
a slow boa
tightening its grip
on the mountain

James Newton

AUTUMN'S KINGDOM

A flock
of blackbirds
beat about
in a gale.
Trees
splinter.
Everywhere,
the empty
eyeholes
of a skull
watch us
closely.

Howie Good

cold crunching down
cleaner streets / warm at home
salt-lined shoes

Harry Giles

mahjong
cloudburst on a tin roof
then
fitful
drips

James Newton

Bird Collides with Window

becoming a dark
hieroglyph
on the dimpled
blank page
of the snow

Andrea Blythe

yellow clouds
of pollen
on the parquet floor
from the bouquet of sunflowers
around which we sit
trying to solve our problems

Eric G. Muller

Winter Breakfast

The last spoonful
of sunlight hits
the leaf covered lawn.

Christian Ward

drinking sangria

thinking of lorca

and the
red
covering the ground

William Wright Harris

between work and home
the only dog that doesn't bark as I walk by
has the saddest eyes

Kuvalaya

millions of stars
in the summer sky--
I walk by myself

Pravat Kumar Padhy

moon
on the waves
night undulates

Máire Morrissey-Cummins

The same rain on my window
as on the wrinkled
face of the man
under the bridge at night.

Samantha Duncan

In my morning rush a cream moon descends in a lavender sky.

Christina Deanne

brief rain—
the tender sound
from leaves

Pravat Kumar Padhy

turning compost
    a bright green leaf
        of brussels sprout

Robert Quiggle III

rose garden
a child searching for
Thumbelina

Christine L. Villa

Five Geese

Out of the mist
in a row of beans
a gardener hears
five geese wing-bellow
low over his bent back.

David Fraser

seed holes.
I say hello to the neighbor
I quarreled with

Melissa Allen

The soft nap grass
brushed by blasts
of sun

      in June.

Jody Porter

SWEETTALK

Hold your hammer, honey, your board, your wood hauled
from the lot for Harry Woodman's saw. Back from the field,
honey, and look what I've got! Smell my fingers, honey, and
look at my full bowl! That tickles licking my fingers, honey,
ain't this some great luck? Pine. Fruit. Fine pickin's, don't you
think, honey?

Patricia Ranzoni

hills lined with slack telephone lines
too heavy for conversations
had given up talk to cicadas
that buzzed with August heat.

Sheri L. Wright

Dried fruit in glass cups
a tea-pot by a nut pie,
autumnal picnic

Claudia Messelodi

White cockatoos stark
against storm glazed skies
summer in Melbourne

Vicki Thornton

The Symbol

A crudely painted swastika
on a park wall. the lichen
around it furious, slowly
covering it from budding trees.

Christian Ward

The strand of her hair
was coiled stark red in the dawn's
new bar of white soap.

Guy Duperreault

In the headlights, wet pavement unfurls—the black tongue of winter.

Kelly Eastlund

TWO RED WINGS

All that's left to glow
of the cardinal

that my across-the-street
neighbor's cat killed

Howie Good

Still watching my step for a tail that sits as ashes on my dresser.

Jessica Negrón

It is a hot day, dry as an old bone,
and suddenly
I want to be swimming,
my shoulders covered in cool water,
my hair solid and dark.

Kathleen Brewin Lewis

on the edge of a leaf
a rain drop contemplates

leaping.

Karuna Chandrashekar

"I'll tell you what love of this life is.
It's looking up
through trees newly bare of leaves
and seeing there the oldest road,
a broken line of white stars
stretching out across the sky.

It's thinking,
this could be enough."
~ Susan Elbe

purple explosion
at end of green fuse —
first crocus

Craig W. Steele

From its high vantage point, on top of an aerial, on top of the pub, a blackbird sings its heart out. Traffic hurtles by on the road below.

A woman walks past with a cat in a basket.

Rosalind Broomhall

a pinprick
of a man,
buffing up
the silvery hat
of a sail-less
windmill

Annie Rapstoff

at the beach two old men,
their stiff-legged dogs

feigning exercise.

Molly Guy

Monuments

'The problem with this country,'
                        he said
'Is we haven't any pyramids.'

Jody Porter

the smell of sagebrush
baking in the sun as we drive across eastern washington
clears the mind
like god's own smudgestick

Lara Simmons

awake

the forest clots
the pond curls

Frog binoculars
the brambled broth

       above

Dan Mussett

Molten pools of pewter mirror sodden skies

Kym Wilson

two days' swansong sun /
quiet litter-strewn sands now
folded up in harr

Harry Giles

A sleeve of rain
moves down the beach,
racing the bathers to their cars.

Kathleen Brewin Lewis

Taiwan mooncake
hangs low in the autumn sky
mother and I
stand on Pacific coasts...
who first has a bite?

Chen-ou Liu

bright calm
hands and knees, water-deep
rake the sand
with thin-skinned hands
bright clam

Beth Balousek

barefoot crew—
you see some
awfully bad
toenails
at sea

M. Kei

Josie says, I want an elegant dress, a painting of an apple that does not taste like paint, and a silence that does not bore me. I want a mind that does not wander. I want everyone to go away and then to come back and then to go away again. I want to tear up these words and rewrite them. May I do that, author?

Jade Bennington

Charity

Some books are best read
standing upright in Oxfam
with rain dripping
from your moustache,
while all the black umbrellas
drip quietly away.

Ian Mullins

This empty cup: You sipped the bad coffee from it, then washed it for me.

Kathy in the Wallowas

first yellow rain —
my newborn son baptizes
the doctor

Craig W. Steele

Big-eyed, beautiful, bedraggled:
a brown-blond child in a navy coat.

Laura Elizabeth Woollett

grocery shopping
mother raids the car trunk on a
ninety degree Monday, looking
for the quinoa.

Amanda Harris

a mesh sack
of garlic, one bulb broken
where it's open

Robert Quiggle III

next door neighbor
plays fetch with our dogs
over the back fence

T.D. Ingram

The deep, spiced cocktail of the hedgerow -
honeysuckle, dogshit, wet grass

Nikki Magennis

Summer heat.
My kitten poses
On the fence.

Alan Zhukovski

her son asks to climb
me like a small tree
I kiss her when
he's not looking because
I'm new here

Lucas Stensland

They laughed when Anna said the real deer may try to mate
with her yard's fake, plastic deer, and there would be a whole
bunch of hybrid offspring born on the doorstep, with plastic
ears and eyes that wouldn't close.

Scott Riley Irvine

Oak and maple leaves gather
at the back door, crinkly
as old paper grocery sacks.

Dried husks of summer's
long days, they beg to be let in
from the cold.

Elizabeth Polkinghorn

shoals of silver-backed
leaves
turning in the wind

Niall O'Connor

on the way to counselling
buds emerging from trees in shadow
remind me of shrapnel
metal wounds blossoming
from flesh

Tammy Hanna

Christmas stocking
a boy pretends
he hasn't caught Santa

Christine L. Villa

Wasps

Painted black and yellow
the broken marionette
takes too long to die.

Laura Elizabeth Woollett

Open the door to the balcony.
I want to smell the leaves
Desperately sticking to the windows
In the boiling storm.

Alan Zhukovski

Vagabonds

I can feel you somehow
you put your hand in the
air when you sleep

the snow falls. The night
is dark.

Annette Anne

The perigee moon,
saffron disc
snared in a net
of black branches.

Margo Roby

the owl
finally sees me
harvest moon

Melissa Allen

winter morning—
little birds arching up
into the blue forever

M. Kei

milk climbs its way through my coffee
like hoarfrost on windows
little fingers reaching out

Corey Hutchins

Antarctica

How small we are
Shades of turquoise
We get close enough
To break off pieces
That melt in our mouth

Lynda Bruce

Dark clouds dump rain on
dozens of sober toned automobiles
the ranunculus yellow Volkswagen
stages a one car happiness sit-in.

Josephine Faith Gibbs

Spring

It has rained.
The long worm

dangles from a yellow beak.

Carson Pierpont

COLORS AMONG GREEN

Flowers?Birds!

Thom Worldpoet

Snow bunting.
White ruffled feathers in heather -
among scabius & crowberries.

Nat Hall

opening the blinds
in autumn light
- the tail of a lizard

Kirsten Nørgaard

out the window
branches form
a jesus fish

Larry Jones

When Night Falls

on a bullet train
I read *Remembrance of Things Past*
outside my soul's window
a dark blue sea

Chen-ou Liu

A friend I've not seen for some weeks sends an email today. Did she want to talk, I query. Instead of replying she tells me about standing in a field of snow, shouting at the sky. The night was dark, the moon was gone. This is what it must feel like, she writes, to stand on the corner of 4th and Exposition holding a cardboard sign: Anything Would Help.

Sherry O'Keefe

sick train the night heron shifts silt for all of us

Alan Summers

Heart tongue.
Small twig of rosebush
bent, broken by the weight of snow
still green.

Clarisssa Jakobsons

Old Man's Beard a cyclist wobbles the length of it

Alan Summers

September -

the last time my father and I shared a cigarette

Chris Vola

windblown shiver
pause-

view of the storm

Meike de Nooy

In the middle of a crowd
of people panicking
over whether they'll make it home,
I stop

and catch a snowflake on my tongue.

Jacquelyn Deighton

FORGOTTEN THINGS

the smell
        of cigarette smoke
and
        the inside
        of your legs—

Phil Lane

I awaken on your front lawn
staring at a cumulonimbus cathedral

William Merricle

STRAND

Cleaning out the boxes,
I came across a strand
of your hair,
not thick enough
to hang myself with

but
not thin enough
to burn
either—

Phil Lane

Before I met this Brazilian neighbour

I never thought
I'd dress up
To do the laundry

Carl-Henrik Björck

ragged hip-hop
still
I read Issa

Christina Nguyen

Moth between window and screen
I'm tired.

Gene Myers

Sweetly After You

On heathered hills
Bent to the winds
Do not forget love.

Dominic Ward

drifting between
shadow and light
leaves on the river

Polona Oblak

month #11

rain and rain and
then some

stars reflected
in musty
brown puddles

dorothee lang

splitting logs at night:
who forgot to close the lid
on the galaxy?

Clark Strand

Ice falls quietly
From Winter's warm plum blossoms.

Guy A. Duperreault

the dog groans
dream-woods dirt on her feet

this milk moon

Angie Werren

How to write *small stones*
in seven days

by
Kaspalita Thompson

One: Go to the world

"Go to the pine if you want to learn about the pine, or to the bamboo if you want to learn about the bamboo. And in doing so, you must leave your subjective preoccupation with yourself... However well phrased your poetry may be, if your feeling is not natural—if the object and yourself are separate – then your poetry is not true poetry but your subjective counterfeit."

~ Basho

- Take the time to really look at something today. Go into the natural world (a park, your garden, your neighbour's garden) and let something catch your eye.
- Examine it.
- Write it down.

In the Cambrian mountains, a keeled over apostrophe of mist floats in front of dark, pine covered slopes.

~ Kaspalita

Two: Look, write, and look again

"Writing can be a useful way to sharpen the mind and connect with the world, but it can also dull our perception, for we all too easily get caught in words and the familiar patterns of our thinking, preventing ourselves from seeing the real things around us...

"We need to keep asking ourselves, "Is what I have written true?" and, "Can I put this more succinctly, more accurately, in more detail?""

~ Caroline Brazier in *Acorns Among the Grass*

- As you go about your day, keep your eyes peeled for something to write about.
- Write down what you have noticed.
- Look at what you have written, and then again at what you noticed.
- Is what you have written accurate? Can you make it more accurate? What colour is the back of the leaf? What other colour is it like?
- Re-write your *small stone*.

Oatcake battlefield: slices of beetroot leaking their blood tainting virginal snow-white cream cheese

~ Fiona

Three: Use all your senses

Shh... What can you hear?

I've read lots of people's beautiful *small stones* and I've noticed that the first thing I do is picture them in my mind's eye.

For me sight is the most predominate sense. I have to make an effort of will to imagine the sound of birds, or rain or cars drifting by. When I write I also think I have a tendency to hone in on the visual aspect first.

Noticing this I want to encourage all of us to be aware with all of our senses, and to try and capture something we might not usually capture in our *stones*.

You could try listening for your *small stone* today, or feeling its texture with your fingers, or noticing its smell drifting before you.

In 'Had I not been awake', Seamus Heaney writes:

"...A wind that rose and whirled until the roof
Pattered with quick leaves off the sycamore"

and I can hear it.

- Notice with your other senses today.
- Write a *small stone* about what you have heard or felt.

A crescent of spilt dark coffee on a white saucer, the crumbled edge of a digestive biscuit, and the clink of a teaspoon meeting the edge of the cup.

~ Kaspalita

Four: Notice a person

Tell me about that person. Not what you think about her or him - but how he or she is.

We so often find in other people what we expect to find. We so often see in other people what we expect to see. Really look today — what is true?

- Pay attention to other people today.
- Write your *small stone* about one of them.
- Make it as specific an observation as possible.

"It is probably impossible to get to a point of seeing the reality of each person, impossible to remove the colouring through which we see the world completely. But it is possible to hold an awareness that real people are complex and interesting and have their own inner lives that we can never fully know. To appreciate the mystery of the other."

~ Kaspalita, from the 'Finding Your Way Home' e-course

in black suit and tie a thin young man with a cherry helmet sits upright on his moped speeding by

~ Carla M. Wilson

Five: Keep going

Doing something everyday can be hard. It's easy to lapse. I'll just finish this email before I write my *small stone*. I just want to watch the end of this movie. I need to sort out the kids' dinner...

Be kind to yourself. Make space to notice the world, and to write every day.

- Notice something.
- Write it down.
- Polish what you have written.

We're on day five. Great work.

> There are rust spots along the edge of the needle. I rub them off with my thumbnail, as best I can, and hold my breath as I push the thread through its eye.
>
> ~ Kaspalita

Six: Peace through writing

We're nearly at the end of this experience. How are you doing?

Putting pen to paper can help me cut through the forest of my own thoughts so that I can really see the world.

The Japanese word *seijaku* is usually translated simply as 'calmness', but perhaps a more accurate translation is 'calmness in the midst of busyness'.

It's easy to be calm when you're on a beach watching the sunset and listening to the waves gently lapping the shore. It's less easy to find that space in the midst of our ordinary working lives. Creating a space for writing poetry in the middle of my busy life helps me to find some calm. Some *seijaku*.

- Pay attention to world
- What springs out at you today?
- Write about it.

light of the moon moves west — flowers' shadows
creep eastward

~ Buson

Seven: Join us and keep writing

1) If you'd like to learn more about using *small stones* to slow down and fall in love with the world, download Fiona Robyn's *How to Write Your Way Home*. It's completely free: www.fionarobyn.com/Howtowriteyourwayhome.pdf

2) Get more engaged with the world by taking one of our month long e-courses.

> "The course met and exceeded my expectations. Fiona's weekly essays, questions and list of resources, as well as her daily emails, provided a wealth of thought provoking material as well as inspiration and support for my writing and life."

> ~ Kath Powell, e-course participant

Find out more: www.writingourwayhome.com/p/e-courses-offerings.html

Most importantly: Keep writing *small stones*. Write in your notebook, or put them on a blog. It will help you slow down and fall in love with the world.

Stay in touch with the *small stones* movement (and Fiona and Kaspa) at www.writingourwayhome.com.

a walk in Dymock:

forget-me-nots star the verges. cows release their
streams of generous urine onto the ground. skylark
song skitters high above. a field of green wheat roils in
the breezes. I brush my fingers across its giant pelt as
we cross from one side to the other. the sky is blue,
blue, blue.

~ Fiona

Acknowledgements

We are hugely grateful to Ruth Feiertag and Ken Hurd for generously donating their time and energy to this project.

Ruth gave the text a thorough proof–reading and editing with accuracy and graciousness. Thank you also to everyone else who read the manuscript and sent suggestions. Any remaining errors are ours and ours alone.

Ken offered to create artwork for the cover after a chance meeting at a Malvern arts fair, and as you can see he's made something very beautiful which does our author's writing proud. Find out more about his work at www.kenhurd.com.

Lightning Source UK Ltd.
Milton Keynes UK
UKOW051630050313

207138UK00003B/4/P